75 Actionable
change the way you think

Good

Books

Gone

Bad

TABLE OF CONTENTS

INTRODUCTION

* We've given this book a fresh new look with an updated and extended version. The interior design has been revamped, and a new table of contents has been added for easy navigation. What's more, this new edition contains 100% of the content from the previous version, plus additional material that builds upon the original. Whether you're a new reader or a returning one, we're confident that you'll find this edition to be an even more engaging and informative read.

INTRODUCTION

Welcome to the world of self-discovery and transformation!

In a world overflowing with information and self-help books, it can be challenging to find the ones that truly have the power to change our lives. We all seek personal growth, happiness, and fulfilment, but sifting through the sea of books can feel like searching for a needle in a haystack. That's why I wrote "Good Books Gone Bad" – to help you find the most impactful insights that will transform the way you think.

Within the pages of this book, we will embark on a journey of self-discovery and transformation. Drawing from the wisdom of hundreds of books during my reading journey, I have carefully curated a collection of actionable insights that delve into personal growth, happiness, mindfulness, human psychology, philosophy, and mental health. **These insights have had a profound impact on my own life, and now I am thrilled to share them with you.**

But first, let's explore the fundamental truth that underlies our entire existence: **the power of thinking**. Our thoughts are the architects of our reality, shaping our perceptions, emotions, actions, and overall well-being. They hold within them the key to unlocking our full potential and living a more meaningful life.

Ancient wisdom, exemplified by the teachings of Buddha, offers profound insights into the significance of our thoughts. Buddha understood the transformative nature of our thinking, expressing that "All that we are is the result of what we have thought." These words resonate across time and space, emphasizing how our thoughts shape our character, actions, and ultimately, our destiny. They lay the foundation for our journey of self-discovery.

Buddha's teachings also highlight the practice of mindfulness, the art of observing our thoughts without judgment. By cultivating awareness of our thought patterns, we can recognize negative or harmful tendencies and consciously redirect them towards positive and beneficial ones. This practice empowers us to take control of our thinking, harness its transformative power, and create a life aligned with our deepest values.

The journey doesn't end there. Another Buddha's profound teaching: "We are what we think. All that we are arises with our thoughts. With our thoughts, we make the world." These words illuminate the creative power inherent in our thinking. Our thoughts shape our perception of reality, influencing our experiences and interactions with the world.

By cultivating a positive and constructive mindset, we open ourselves to a world of endless possibilities. Our thinking not only impacts our internal state but also how we perceive and respond to external circumstances. It becomes the catalyst for a more fulfilling and purposeful life, benefiting not only ourselves but also those around us.

"Good Books Gone Bad: 75 Actionable Insights That Will Change the Way You Think" is your guide to unleashing the power of thought and action for lasting transformation. **Each chapter reveals actionable insights that have the potential to reshape your thinking and, consequently, your life.**

Unlike most nonfiction books that have one point to make (they make it and then they give you example after example after example after example, and they apply it to explain everything in the world), this book cuts through the clutter and presents only the most valuable and practical insights.

Let's be honest, not all self-help books are created equal. There are the gems that truly changed my life, and then there are the duds that just took up my time. That's why I wrote "Good Books Gone Bad", to share the best of the best with you.

You have the freedom to navigate through this book as you wish. Dive into the chapters that resonate with you the most, exploring the topics that ignite your curiosity and fuel your desire for growth. As you absorb each insight, you'll find yourself expanding your knowledge, embracing a growth mindset, and cultivating a positive attitude towards personal growth and learning.

So, are you ready to embark on this transformative journey? Are you prepared to challenge your current thinking patterns and open yourself up to new possibilities? If so, then "Good Books Gone Bad" is your key to unlocking the door to a life of fulfilment and meaningful change.

Let's embark on this adventure together. The path to transformation begins now!

*If you're ready to take your self-discovery to the next level, I encourage you to pick up the books that inspired each chapter and delve even deeper into those topics. (Check the additional resources at the end of the book)

PART 1: HAPPINESS AND MINDFULNESS

Life is just a series of present moments

Have you ever thought about the two emotions that hold us back the most? If you asked 100 people, chances are, most of them would say regret and anxiety. But why do we worry so much?

The answer lies in the way our minds work. Our constant stream of thoughts is usually focused on either the past or the future. Take oversleeping for example, we might start by regretting hitting the snooze button and then worry about being late for work.

However, **the most crucial time is the one we often neglect: the present**. It's the only moment where everything happens - all our emotions and actions.

"Realize deeply that the present moment is all you have. Make the NOW the primary focus of your life." - Eckhart Tolle

The past is simply a collection of past present moments, and the future is just a bunch of present moments yet to come.

So, it's pointless to live in any moment other than the present. If you have a research paper due in 14 days, all the time you spend regretting procrastination or worrying about the workload ahead won't get you any closer to your goal.

Focus on the present and start solving your problem right now, and you'll be on your way to making progress. Embrace the power of the present, and see how it can change your life!

"The more you are focused on time - past and future - the more you miss the Now, the most precious thing there is."
- Eckhart Tolle

Live in the now

Dwelling on the past usually results in regret, which you cannot change. Worrying about the future only adds to your anxiety about something you can't control.

We can only live in the present moment, so try to concentrate on that.

We can learn to live more fully in the world around us by staying present and understanding that we are not our thoughts.

One dart hurts enough - but you'll worsen your pain if you dwell on it

Much of our pain is felt on two different levels:

The first level is similar to being hit by a dart: a sudden rush of pain. It could be the result of an accident, such as stubbing your toe, touching a hot plate, or crashing your bike, or it could be the result of a failed expectation, failure, or rejection.

This type of suffering is unavoidable. We all have to deal with it at some point in our lives, and there isn't much we can do about it.

However, **most of the time, we aggravate the situation by throwing a second dart at ourselves based on how we physically and mentally react to the first.**

All of this adds to our suffering, except the fact that we have complete control over it. **This type of pain is entirely optional.**

Instead, we must learn to accept the pain, do what needs to be done to heal our wounds, and move on with our lives.

The second darts are usually more painful than the first because we keep throwing them throughout the aftermath, often long after the first dart has vanished.

For example, we may obsess for months over a failed relationship or worry through countless sleepless nights about test results.

Why would we throw more darts at ourselves when life already throws enough at us?

Endure your pain, end your suffering.

Recognize when something causes you pain. Recognize how it makes you feel and wait for the pain to go away. Do not aggravate the situation by becoming angry or upset with any other factors or people involved.

"Only we humans worry about the future, regret the past, and blame ourselves for the present." - Rick Hanson

The philosophy of stoicism argues the idea that the only pain you really suffer is the one you create yourself.

All pain stems from resistance to things you can't change. Negative events happen all the time for reasons beyond our control. We can, however, choose how we respond to them.

Pain is simply the result of your resistance to everything you are powerless to change.

We spend a lot of time thinking about the future and the past, but we can only live in the present and thus have no way of changing many things that make us unhappy.

To fill the void, **we develop a resistance to these things, which we perceive as psychological or physical pain.**

When we're angry or upset, we think and act more irrationally, which almost always results in a worse situation. As a result, our reactions to things over which we have no control can perpetuate the pain cycle.

"All negativity is caused by an accumulation of psychological time and denial of the present." - Eckhart Tolle

Acknowledge your pain in resistance.

We all replay events from our past in our minds. This causes us psychological pain because we resist what we can't change when all we can do is fix or move on. Recognize your pain and then move on.

"A man who fears suffering is already suffering from what he fears." - Montaigne

You can free yourself from pain by constantly observing your mind and not judging your thoughts

How can you get rid of your distress? There are two choices. First, regularly ask yourself: "What will my next thought be? Second, stop judging your thoughts and desires.

The first strategy is based on a physics effect known as the Quantum Zeno effect, which states that by constantly observing a system, you can freeze it in its current state.

Repeatedly asking yourself about your next thought will usually delay that thought, giving you enough time to realize how much time you actually spend on autopilot. You can begin the process of separating from your mind by interrupting it.

The second method is intended to help you learn to listen to your body and accept the constant, nagging thoughts in your head about what you should or should not be doing.

The next time you make a mistake, simply listen to your inner voice and don't act on it. Notice it, see it, accept that it exists, but resist its demands.

Separating your body from your constantly active, thought-driven mind will allow you to feel less pain and stop resisting what you can't change.

"Stay present, and continue to be the observer of what is happening inside you. Become aware not only of the emotional pain but also of 'the one who observes,' the silent watcher. This is the power of the Now, the power of your own conscious presence." - Eckhart Tolle

Acknowledge your own thought process.

You can stop your own thought process if you can consciously observe it. Concentrate on concentrating rather than allowing your mind to wander, and you will gain control.

Don't be so harsh on yourself.

Don't punish yourself when you do something wrong or fail to do something when you should have. What has been done is done. Recognize your accomplishment and take a deep breath. Allow it to wash over you and then move on. All you can do is study.

Quit the eternal rat race and practice composure every day

Most of us tend to use the concept of 'composure' incorrectly. When we say it, we expect to act without expressing our emotions.

Assume you are a student who receives an email in the middle of class informing you that you have been accepted to your top choice school. You'll probably want to get up right away.

However, if you do, your teacher will simply tell you to "keep it together." But **keeping your cool doesn't mean you have to hide your emotions.**

Staying with your feelings for just long enough to let them sink in, but without developing a permanent reaction to them, is what composure entails.

When it comes to maintaining composure, it's all about being mindful of your emotions. Allow yourself to fully feel them, but don't let them take hold of you permanently.

It's great to bask in a well-deserved victory, but the true test of your emotional stability is when you can move past it and not get consumed by the need for more.

Composure acts as a reset button, disconnecting the thought patterns of, "I'm on top of the world," and "I need more success at any cost."

The same goes for when we experience negative emotions, breaking the connection between, "I'm feeling down," and "I must avoid similar situations in the future."

We can practice true composure by paying attention to when we are feeling particularly good or bad and then taking a brief moment to simply be with the sensation.

During this time, we allow the sensation to sink in while accepting that everything is fine as it is. We don't have to start chasing the next thought in our heads right away.

Acknowledge your feelings.

Embracing your emotions is key!

Instead of pushing them down, give yourself permission to fully experience them. Take a moment to be present with your feelings, whether they are joyful, angry, or heartbroken.

Let them sink in and remember, it's okay to feel!

We can reduce suffering in life by not associating ourselves with material objects

Embrace the art of letting go like a Buddhist Monk!

By letting go, they have the power to transform suffering into peace, fulfillment, and acceptance.

Even in the face of death, the choice to let go can bring about a sense of tranquility instead of lingering on pain.

Having a strong sense of self is important, but there's a fine line between having a sense of identity and getting too attached. Yes, our sense of self gives us purpose in life and sets us apart from others, but running away to live in the woods is not the answer.

Instead, we can cultivate a healthy sense of self by letting go of the things we attach our identities to.

Every time we say "my" or "I" in regards to something, we give it power over us.

As everything in this world eventually comes to an end, over-identifying with things can lead to a constant feeling of loss and even depression. Think about all the things we say "my" to – our clothes, electronics, possessions – and imagine if they all break down over time.

The more we attach our sense of self to material objects, the more potential we have for feelings of sadness and gloom. **Try decluttering for a weekend and see how it can help regulate your sense of self.**

And remember, as you step out into the world, look up to the highest building in sight and imagine seeing yourself from a bird's eye view. Keep zooming out until you see the bigger picture, just like on Google Maps.

You're just a small part of this vast universe, so why let material possessions bring you stress and sorrow?

Be happy just being yourself.

Although confronting your problems can be frightening, and there can be a lot of pressure to conform to what others expect of you, being yourself in its purest form can bring you the most peace and happiness.

Have a clear out.

Although your material possessions can provide you with temporary happiness, **excessive ownership** can cause you distress when it breaks, is lost, or makes a mess. Declutter your life by getting rid of unnecessary possessions.

You don't have to be religious in order to be spiritual

Ditch the labels and embrace your own path to spirituality!

The Dalai Lama says it doesn't matter if you're a part of a religion or not, **what's important is that you're a compassionate and kind-hearted person.**

There's no one-size-fits-all approach when it comes to dealing with life's big questions and handling suffering.

Whether it's through meditation, religion, or finding meaning in life's experiences, embrace the method that works best for you.

Don't let anyone tell you what's right or wrong when it comes to spirituality. The way you choose to connect with your beliefs is entirely up to you, so take a moment to reflect on what being spiritual means to you. It's your journey, so own it!

"Life is long if you know how to use it."
- Seneca

Discover the practices that make you closer to happiness.

It's easy to become so engrossed in our daily lives that we lose sight of how brief life can be.

Certain practices are followed by believers in every religion and spiritual belief to bring them closer to true happiness.

Practicing something, even if it's just a movement, can help you ground yourself and reach new levels of consciousness. Focus on actions rather than just beliefs.

Life's only constant is change

When asked about suffering, The Dalai Lama cautions against the common Western misconception that suffering is abnormal and something to be avoided at all costs.

He asserts that suffering is a natural part of life and by denying it, we only bring more pain upon ourselves.

The truth is, change is the only constant in life and holding on tightly to what we know only leads to more suffering.

The key is to embrace change, not resist it!

By accepting that life is in a constant state of flux, we can open ourselves up to the lessons and growth that come with it.

"We suffer more in imagination than in reality." - Seneca

Instead of complaining about a slammed car door or a slow cashier, we can find the silver lining and turn the situation around. And when faced with heartache from a breakup, we can find the strength to move forward.

Embracing change and letting go is the path to true happiness.

Embrace a state of acceptance.

What we resist persists!

When a painful event occurs, accept the pain and sorrow that it brings.

Resisting it will only exacerbate the feelings and pain.

We gain clarity and move closer to happiness when we let go of control.

"One moment can change a day, one day can change a life and one life can change the world." - Buddha

Know your limits

Discovering your confidence starts with being true to yourself. The Dalai Lama suggests we embrace our limitations and be honest about what we can and can't do.

Instead of trying to fake it until you make it, openly admit when you're not sure about something and watch how quickly people come to your aid.

Honesty is not just the best policy, but it also gives others an opportunity to help you and build you up.

When you're open and honest about your limitations, you're inviting others to come alongside you and support you, building a sense of community and solidarity.

Being aware of your limitations and embracing them also leads to a greater sense of self-awareness. This means taking a deep dive into your strengths and weaknesses, so you can focus your energy on what you're good at, and seek help in areas you need improvement in.

This self-awareness will lead you down a path of personal growth and development, helping you **build confidence from the inside out.**

So, embrace your limits, be honest about what you can and can't do, trust yourself and trust the journey, and watch as you become a more confident, self-assured person, ready to tackle whatever challenges come your way.

Journal to get to know yourself better.

Putting things down on paper always provides us with a sense of clarity. If you want to achieve happiness, you must first understand what it means to you.

Make a list of everything. What do you require and desire from life? How do you intend to accomplish it?

Suffering is inevitable in life, but that doesn't mean you should increase it

Life is tough, and no one can deny that. It's natural to suffer sometimes, but the truth is, most of us make it even harder by clinging to poor values.

We chase fleeting pleasures, like wild parties or reckless relationships, instead of looking for true and long-lasting satisfaction.

Or we become obsessed with material possessions, thinking that we'll finally be happy once we've acquired them all.

But research shows that beyond a certain point, wealth and success have little to do with our overall well-being. We need to shift our priorities and focus on what really matters.

The most fulfilling purpose in life is to make the world a better place, not just for ourselves, but for everyone around us. When we contribute to the greater good, we experience a sense of meaning and fulfillment that can't be found in self-centered pursuits.

And that includes our spending habits. Instead of mindlessly buying the latest gadget or trend, we should be mindful of how we use our resources to improve our own lives and the lives of others.

So, let's rethink our values and start living a life that's not only meaningful but also genuinely happy.

"Happiness is not a solvable equation. Dissatisfaction and unease are Inherent parts of human nature and necessary components to creating consistent happiness." - Mark Manson

Pleasure and enjoyment are two different things

"When a person can't find deep sense of meaning, they distract themselves with pleasure." - Victor Frankl

Say goodbye to confusing pleasure with happiness!

Today, people are often mistaken about the source of their happiness, but the truth is, pleasure and happiness are two very different things.

While **pleasure** is derived from fleeting sensory experiences such as indulging in a delicious meal or receiving a relaxing massage, it ultimately takes control away from you and your attention.

True happiness, however, comes from **enjoyment**, which requires focus and conscious engagement. By bringing your attention to the present moment, you regain control and can actively work towards your most important goals.

Sadly, our fast-paced, instant gratification-focused society often prioritizes pleasure over enjoyment, leading many to feel unfulfilled and unhappy.

But the good news is, you can tap into true happiness by seeking out opportunities for **flow - a state of deep focus and engagement**. So, let's embrace enjoyment and leave pleasure behind!

Be aware of pleasure over enjoyment.

Before you spend your money on something you truly desire. Consider whether it will provide you with pleasure or enjoyment.

If the former, save your money for something less materialistic that will bring you genuine, long-lasting happiness.

"A joyful life is an individual creation that cannot be copied from a recipe."

- Mihaly Csikszentmihalyi

Flow is where challenges and skills match

Dive into the world of ultimate enjoyment with the power of "flow"!

Have you ever been so absorbed in an activity that time just flies by? That's flow - the state of total immersion and pure bliss where all your worries disappear.

Attaining this euphoric state can be achieved through two simple steps:

1. Choose an activity that you're passionate about and do it just for the love of it, without any external motivation like money or fame.

2. Ensure that the level of challenge in the activity is perfectly balanced, not too easy or too difficult, but just right.

To find your flow, focus on doing something that's meaningful and enjoyable to you. Don't let external factors like money or fame cloud your experience.

For the second step, gradually build up the challenge level of the activity. If you're learning a new game like chess, start with an easier level and gradually increase the challenge as you get better.

By following these steps, you'll experience life as a never-ending game filled with excitement, fulfillment, and happiness. So, go ahead, find your flow and keep the good times rolling!

Find your flow.

Choose a rewarding activity, big or small, that you really enjoy and want to do more of.

Make sure it's not too difficult to begin with, and keep adjusting the difficulty to keep yourself challenged.

"Who chases two rabbits catches neither." - Japanese Proverb

Happiness is a human construct and it doesn't really exist

Western society has bought into the happiness myth - that we need to constantly chase our desires to attain true joy. But in reality, this **never-ending pursuit** only leads to temporary satisfaction and a constant craving for something more.

The truth is that happiness can't be bought or achieved through external means. It's an internal state of being that requires hard work and dedication to a meaningful purpose.

Buddha recognized this cycle of desire and unfulfillment long ago, and his teachings still hold relevance today.

We don't need to become Buddhists to understand the value of his message in a world that is obsessed with chasing success.

So instead of constantly striving for more, let's shift our focus to solving problems and working towards a greater purpose. When we do this, true happiness will naturally follow.

Solve problems that you have stacked up and find your natural high.

Don't let procrastination get in the way of your happiness!

Tackle the small problems you've been avoiding, whether it's fixing your old bike or visiting your relatives. Once you start solving these little problems, you'll find that you feel a sense of accomplishment and a boost in your mood.

And when you have free time, use it wisely!

Instead of falling into the boredom trap of scrolling social media or binge-watching TV shows, find a new hobby to explore. Whether it's cooking, drawing, or learning a new language, engaging in a new activity can be an incredibly fulfilling experience that brings you genuine joy.

So, don't be afraid to step outside of your comfort zone and try something new!

"Who you are is defined by what you are willing to struggle for." - Mark Manson

Life goals are irrelevant, so set a life goal

Are you ready to create a life filled with purpose and meaning? It all starts with setting your sights on an ultimate goal - something that drives you, motivates you, and keeps you in a state of flow.

Your goal doesn't have to be grand or ambitious, as long as it's important to you. It's your personal guide, helping you determine what matters most, what you want to achieve, and how you plan on making it happen.

But remember, **your life goal doesn't define you as a person, it simply serves as a tool to keep you moving forward. And don't be afraid to adapt or change your goal as you grow and evolve - it's all part of the journey.**

Embrace your destiny by taking control of your own story, and keep pushing yourself to grow and challenge yourself. With a clear ultimate goal in mind, the possibilities for your life are endless!

Write down a bucket list.

A bucket list is a simple tool that can assist you in determining your life goal. What are the connections between all of the items on your list? Do they all lead to something bigger? Examine it and draw your own conclusions.

FREE GOODWILL: He who said money can't buy happiness, hasn't given enough money

People who selflessly help others experience increased levels of satisfaction, longer lifespans, and greater financial gains. I'd like to create the opportunity to deliver this value to you as you read. To accomplish this, I have a simple question:

Would you be willing to help an unknown individual if it didn't cost you money?

If your answer is yes, I have a request on behalf of someone you don't know and probably never will. They are just like you (or me) or were like you a few years ago: less experienced, driven to make a positive change in their lives, willing to learn, and seeking guidance but unsure where to find it... and this is where you can step in.

At Bookreadersclub, our mission is to assist people in selecting the right book based on their interests, initiating their journey of self-transformation and personal growth by connecting with them.

As a matter of fact, many individuals do judge a book by its cover and reviews. **If you have found this book valuable thus far, would you please spare a moment now to leave an honest review of the book and its**

contents? It won't cost you any money and will take less than 60 seconds.

Your assistance will help:

...another reader explore their interests
...another beginner discover the perfect book
...another person commence their journey of self-transformation
...another life experience positive change.

To make this possible, all you need to do is... and it won't take more than 60 seconds... leave a review on Amazon.

Thank you sincerely from the depths of my heart. Now, let's return to our regular Insights.

PART 2: HABITS AND PERSONAL GROWTH

When you come up with a new life goal, immediately turn it into a daily habit

Shifting gears towards your dreams can be a challenge, but with the right mindset, you can make it happen!

Have you ever felt stuck in a rut, unable to reach your goals despite your best intentions? It happens to the best of us. But the good news is, change is always within reach.

"Motivation is what gets you started. Habit is what keeps you going" - Jim

Think of your progress as a graph. The more effort you put into making a change, the steeper the upward trajectory. But beware, it's not a one-time solution. Devoting your entire life to a goal is unsustainable.

The key is to find a balance between your new pursuit and the rest of your life. And the secret ingredient? Habits!

Transform your aspirations into a small, daily routine.

For instance, if healthy eating is on your mind, swap your afternoon Snickers bar with an apple. If writing is your passion, start with 250 words a day. And if you're looking for love, send a message to someone new every day.

Finding the right habit that works for you may take some trial and error, but once you do, you'll find it easier to stick with your new practice. So, don't give up, keep experimenting and keep striving towards your dreams.

Repeat until it sticks.

Humans are habitual creatures. The more you do something, the more natural it will become for you to do it.

When beginning a new endeavor, break it down into chunks and practice at least once a day.

"The journey of a thousand miles begins with a single step." - Lao Tzu

It's much easier to build new habits when you make them obvious and attractive

"Good habits formed at youth make all the difference." - Aristotle

Let's talk about building better habits. The first rule of thumb is to make your habits obvious, so that you're able to easily spot which actions are helping or hindering you.

By becoming aware of your daily routines, you can identify both the positive and negative habits that shape your life. Making your bed each morning is an example of a positive habit, whereas eating a chocolate bar every day when trying to lose weight is a negative one.

"The process of behavior change always starts with awareness." - James Clear

To establish new, positive habits, you need to focus on the time and location of the behavior. By choosing a specific time and place to perform the habit, you're more likely to stick with it.

For instance, if you want to work out at 6 p.m. every day, you should make sure to do it in the same location, creating a routine.

But it's not just about establishing habits - they also have to be attractive. Habits are driven by dopamine, which gives us the motivation to keep going. To make a habit attractive, try pairing it with something you enjoy doing.

For example, if you love watching Netflix, but need to exercise more, try watching your favorite show only when you're on the treadmill.

By making your habits obvious and attractive, you can create a foundation for a healthier and happier life.

"It is the anticipation of a reward - not the fulfillment of it - that gets us to take action." - James Clear

Changes that seem small and unimportant at first will compound into remarkable results if you're willing to stick with them for years

The foundations for each habit you have follows a simple, easily managed formula:

James Clear, a renowned author, has taken Pulitzer Prize-winning journalist Charles Duhigg's The Power of Habit to the next level by providing a better understanding of how habits form and how to develop new ones.

Every habit has four essential components that contribute to its formation:

The first is the "**cue**," a signal that triggers the habit. The second is the "**craving**," a desire to fulfill the habit. The third is the "**response**," the actual habit, and the fourth is the "**reward**," the gratification that results from completing the habit.

For instance, if you receive a notification on your phone, it serves as your cue. You then crave to find out what it is, resulting in your response, where you open your phone and access the notification, which is your reward. With time, this routine can become a habit, and you may find yourself checking your phone whenever it vibrates, without any conscious thought.

This "Habit Loop" is common to both positive and negative habits, and it can be difficult to break out of. However, by understanding the four components of a habit, you can develop new habits that can help you achieve your goals.

Habits are the foundation of your identity, and to change them, you must begin by asking yourself who you want to be.

Your identity is shaped by repeated actions, and by improving yourself by just 1% every day, you can make significant changes to your life.

Just as one paint-by-numbers does not make you an artist, one day of positive habits does not define you. However, with consistency, you can create a daily routine that will help you become the person you want to be.

Make small daily changes to reap long-term rewards.

Believing that you need to make significant changes to your life to adopt new habits is a misconception. Instead, focus on making small adjustments and improvements gradually each day. Over time, these incremental changes will accumulate, leading to long-lasting positive effects.

If you want new behaviors to become lasting habits, make them both easy and satisfying to accomplish

Let's talk about the easy route to creating new habits. We all know that when it comes to achieving something, we're often drawn to the path of least resistance. If we make something easy, we're more likely to do it.

For example, if you want to learn to play the guitar, keeping it by the sofa means that you're more likely to pick it up and strum a few chords.

The opposite is also true for bad habits. If we make something difficult or awkward to do, we're less likely to do it.

That's where **the two-minute rule** comes in handy. Most habits are formed at a specific moment, and if we can accomplish them quickly, we're more likely to stick to them.

For instance, if you want to go for a run every morning, laying your clothes and trainers out the night before will make it easier to start.

The key to lasting change is to take small steps and make progress every day.

The fourth law of behavior change focuses on making new habits satisfying.

A habit tracker can help you keep track of your progress and give you a sense of pride and satisfaction. If you're writing a book, for example, jotting down your daily word count can help you finish it faster.

But we're all wired to crave immediate rewards, and that's where the power of positive reinforcement comes in. Attach a positive reward to your new habit, and you're more likely to stick to it.

If you're trying to cut down on eating out, save the money you would have spent and treat yourself to a new jacket or a holiday. That way, you get an instant reward for sticking to your new habit.

"Each day is made up of many moments, but it is really a few habitual choices that determine the path you take." - James clear

Wake up early and use the 20/20/20 formula

Are you tired of waking up early only to spend the extra time scrolling through social media or watching the news? It's time to optimize your mornings with the perfect plan.

"One day you will wake up and there won't be any more time to do things you've always wanted. Do it now."
- Paulo Coelho

According to Robin Sharma's 20/20/20 rule, the first hour of your day should consist of three highly valuable activities. Here's how you can use the rule to your advantage:

Start with 20 minutes of exercise to awaken your body and get those endorphins flowing. Sweating not only reduces stress and fear but also releases Brain-Derived Neurotrophic Factor (BDNF), a crucial factor for improving your cognitive abilities.

Next, spend 20 minutes in reflection, taking the peace of the morning to find inspiration. Write down your thoughts and focus on what you want out of the day ahead.

Follow that up with meditation, which has been shown to reduce cortisol and stress levels.

Finally, dedicate your last 20 minutes to learning. Read a book, listen to a podcast, or work on a new skill. The key to success is a love of learning.

But it doesn't stop there. By cultivating a morning routine that works for you, you can start each day off on the right foot. Prioritize sleep by having some screen-free hours before bed, keeping a regular routine, and ensuring you get enough sleep for your body.

Embrace the day and make the most of your mornings with these simple tips.

Prioritize sleep.

Having a restful sleep is essential to kickstarting your day early. To achieve this, make sure to disconnect from your screens at least a few hours before bedtime, establish a regular sleep routine, and ensure that you're getting enough sleep for your body's needs.

Create a routine you can stick to, so you won't lose your momentum

Imagine a snowball rolling down a hill, gathering more and more snow with each turn, until it becomes an unstoppable force. That's the power of momentum in action!

The same concept applies to our daily habits and routines. The more positive habits you develop, the easier it becomes to make good decisions, until they become second nature to you.

Think of it as building up your own personal "Big Mo." With enough momentum, you'll feel unstoppable!

The only catch is getting that momentum started. It can be difficult to form a new habit, but the key is to focus on consistency over perfection.

"Procrastination will delay your dreams"

- Vex King

For example, if your goal is to hit the gym three times a week, start by simply showing up, even if you only complete a short workout. Consistency will help turn that habit into a routine. So, let's get rolling and start building our own unstoppable momentum!

Don't break your momentum.

Your habit must be prioritized on your to-do list.

Missing a few sessions is all it takes to break the cycle - and render all your efforts ineffective.

"You will never change your life until you change the habits you do daily. The secret of your success is found in your daily routine." - Darren Hardy

Use momentum to push through your limits, even if you have to trick yourself at first

When you're pushing towards your limits, it's important to have the power of momentum on your side.

That's why developing a good routine is so critical - it'll give you the boost you need to break through the barriers that are holding you back.

Your good habits and decisions will start to compound and carry you forward with increasing force.

Of course, even the strongest of us will reach a limit eventually. When that happens, you can use the momentum you've built up to give you an extra boost.

Just like Arnold Schwarzenegger did when he hit his weightlifting limits. He found ways to activate more muscle groups by leaning back slightly, and was able to add an extra five or six reps to his sets.

The same can be true for your weight loss journey, your running routine, or even your writing practice. Try changing up your approach - have water for dinner, take a less steep route for your run, or write an extra page about a different topic. These "cheats" can help you push past your limits and create even more momentum.

Let momentum build up before you give it a boost.

After you've been practicing a habit for a while, you'll need a good push to keep going.

To give yourself the illusion of greater progress, make your practice easier than usual.

Your achievements will speak for themselves.

"If you are serious about changing your life, you'll find a way. If not, you'll find an excuse." - Jen Sincero

You need to stop trying so hard to save time

Are you feeling overwhelmed by the demands of time? Do you find yourself constantly trying to be more productive, only to end up with even longer to-do lists?

It's time to break free from the constraints of clock-driven schedules and embrace a new approach to time management.

Contrary to popular belief, time as a concept does not actually exist. Our perceptions of time are shaped by external forces like clocks, jobs, and deadlines, but they are only real in a collective sense.

The medieval peasant lived a life structured by the tasks they needed to perform, rather than by the clock. It wasn't until the evolution of industrial capitalism that the pressure to make better use of time at work and in leisure became a pressing issue.

So, what's the solution to feeling like there's not enough time in the day? Do less. Focusing on the truly important tasks at hand and letting go of the pressure to be constantly productive will lead to a clearer mind and a lighter workload.

Remember, the average human lifespan is tragically short. which averages around 4,000 weeks.

But that doesn't mean you should live in fear of wasting time. It's a call to action to live life to the fullest and focus on what truly matters.

Trying to master your time paradoxically leads to you being mastered by time.

"The average human lifespan is absurdly, terrifyingly, insultingly short. But that isn't a reason for unremitting despair, or for living in an anxiety-fueled panic about making the most of your limited time. It's a cause for relief." - Oliver Burkeman

Keep two to-do lists.

Make productivity a fixed volume task by keeping two to-do lists, one for each open task and one for the number of tasks you will work on at any given time. Only move tasks from the larger list to the smaller list after completing a task on the latter.

Limit your working time.

Set a time limit for working during the day whenever possible.

Doing more means having to do even more

Many productivity experts advocate achieving 'inbox zero,' or that blissful state of being. Yet, often, this leads to a never-ending cycle of email replies, leading to more emails, leading to more replies.

Becoming a reliable responder can turn into a trap, with more people reaching out to you.

And at work, being seen as a highly productive employee can result in a barrage of additional tasks being thrown your way. But, let's face it, focusing on one task means letting go of an infinite number of other possibilities.

Instead of striving for maximum productivity, let's embrace the art of prioritization. Accept that there will always be tasks left undone and choose to procrastinate on the less important ones. After all, **the key to success is not to do more, but to do what truly matters.**

Get your priorities straight.

Concentrate on only one major task at a time.

Don't let completing minor tasks keep you from focusing on what's truly important.

Underachieve, strategically.

Determine ahead of time which areas of your work and life you will no longer expect perfection in order to make them easier to complete.

"Convenience culture seduces us into imagining that we might find room for everything important by eliminating only life's tedious tasks. But it's a lie. You have to choose a few things, sacrifice everything else, and deal with the inevitable sense of loss that results."
- Oliver Burkeman

Time is a network good

When it comes to things like money and oil, more is always better. Quantity is the name of the game and the more you have, the more valuable it becomes.

But, with network goods, it's a different story. The value of these goods lies in the connections and coordination with others.

Take the telephone for example, the more people you have on the line, the more valuable the device becomes. And with social media, the platform is only as useful as the number of friends and contacts you have on it.

Having plenty of time is desirable, but it's not much good if you're spending it all alone.

The most meaningful experiences in life - spending time with loved ones, building relationships, starting a business, pursuing passion projects - all require coordination and collaboration with others.

Having lots of time but not being able to share it with others is not only a waste of time, but it can also lead to feelings of loneliness and isolation.

"Traditional nomads aren't solitary wanderers who just happen to lack laptops; they're intensely group-focused people... And in their more candid moments, digital nomads will admit that the chief problem with their lifestyle is acute loneliness." - Oliver Burkeman

Focus on your relationships.

Instead of trying to control the outcomes of your personal and professional relationships, become curious about them. Demanding a specific outcome causes stress; wondering what might happen next causes the opposite effect.

Cultivate generosity.

When you think of something generous to do, do it right away rather than allowing it to become yet another unfinished task that adds to your to-do list and causes anxiety. It feels good to give.

The main thing is to keep the main thing the main thing

Learn the 7 Habits of Highly Effective People for actionable steps to improve your habits and become the person you want to be. Whether it's workplace issues, family conflicts, or unsatisfying relationships, anyone can learn to solve and improve interpersonal problems with new habits.

The first three habits are:

- **Be Proactive,**
- **Begin with the End in Mind, and**
- **Put First Things First.**

Life has a way of shaping us, but it doesn't have to control us. While we can't control the actions of others, we can take responsibility for our own reactions, behaviors, and decisions. By being proactive and taking initiative, we can shift our patterns and see the world in a new way.

To be effective in work, play, or relationships, we need clear goals. By reverse-engineering the desired outcome, individuals, organizations, and businesses can work proactively toward a mission. And by remembering that life is finite, we can focus on what really matters: our relationships and legacy.

But distractions are everywhere, from notifications to emails. To form new habits, we need to **learn to prioritize and say no to trivial distractions** - and even worthwhile activities that divert our attention from our goals. If you want to write a book, for instance, it might mean giving up other pursuits in the short term.

Write out your mission statement.

You can put words to your goals and better understand what to focus on by defining what you want to achieve in your chosen area.

Write down what's most important to you and the steps you need to take to get there.

Schedule your priorities in advance.

Set aside 30 minutes, perhaps on a Friday or Sunday, to plan out your week. Set aside specific time slots for your top priorities and don't reschedule them.

"Knowledge is the theoretical paradigm, the what to do. Skill is the how to do. And desire is the motivation, the want to do. In order to make something a habit in our lives, we have to have all three."
- Stephen R. Covey

We're more effective when we consider one another

"Balance what you want with what others want. Be courageous. And considerate." - Stephen R. Covey

Think Win-Win

Life is often thought of as a zero-sum game, where one person must lose for another to win. But what if we told you that working together for everyone's benefit is more profitable in the long run?

Research shows that cooperation instead of competition, focusing on a 'win/win' scenario instead of a 'win/lose,' will increase productivity at work and improve personal relationships. It's all about finding a way for everyone to win.

To achieve this, effective communication is key. We often prioritize making ourselves understood instead of understanding others, but empathic listening is crucial.

Seek First to Understand, Then Be Understood.

And when it comes to forming better habits, tackling one at a time may not be enough. By developing a habit of **synergy**, we can incorporate multiple good habits into our lives simultaneously. This leads to positive and collaborative interactions, and healthy and interdependent relationships

"The challenge is to apply the principles of creative cooperation, which we learn from nature, in our social interactions."
- Stephen R. Covey

Learn to listen.

Resist the urge to offer advice right away! People are most valued when they are simply listened to. Give others your undivided attention and practice empathy.

"We have two ears and one mouth, so we should listen more than we say." - Zeno

No good habit will stick if you're not taking care of yourself

Stephen Covey's seventh habit, "Sharpen the Saw if you want to keep sewing," is the glue that holds all other habits together. It's the ultimate self-care habit that's critical for your well-being.

It's the habit of self-care and self-renewal.

Think of it as maintaining your car so that it runs smoothly on the road. Similarly, you need to take care of yourself to be efficient and effective in all areas of your life.

Whether you're working towards a massive goal or just trying to survive a hectic week, constantly pushing yourself without taking a break can lead to burnout.

To stay in balance, you need to replenish four essential tanks - **emotional, mental, spiritual, and physical**. Make time for exercise, nourishing food, and adequate rest, and don't underestimate the importance of taking time alone to reflect and recharge.

Incorporating "Sharpen the Saw" habit into your life is the most crucial thing you can do to improve your overall well-being. Remember, **you are your most significant asset, so take care of yourself, and you'll be ready to take on the world.**

Proactively practice self-care.

Make time for yourself, whether it's 15 minutes before work or one evening a week.

Rest, eat healthily, and meditate. Relax and engage in your hobbies.

"The goal is not to be better than the other man, but your previous self."

- Dalai Lama

Thinking too much might paralyze you, so just start moving

"Inaction breeds doubt and fear. Action breeds confidence and courage."
- Dale Carnegie

Who Moved My Cheese is a bestselling parable that teaches us to embrace change and thrive in uncertainty. It follows the story of two little people and two mice in a maze searching for cheese, each character representing a different attitude toward change and success.

In Spencer Johnson's parable, two mice named Sniff and Scurry are on a mission to find cheese within a confusing maze. They waste no time in their search and simply follow their instincts, without overthinking.

Meanwhile, two humans named Hem and Haw also search for cheese, but they become bogged down with worries about the future, second-guessing their choices, and feeling anxious about whether there's any cheese left to find.

The lesson to be learned here is that sometimes, simplicity and taking action without excessive analysis can be the key to success. Don't let fear of the unknown or **analysis paralysis** hold you back from finding your own version of "cheese" in life.

Every minute you spend wondering what success looks like, how to achieve it, whether it's even possible, and how you'll feel in the future is a minute you're not working towards.

Like Sniff and Scurry, sometimes it's best to simply follow your instincts and keep moving forward.

Get moving.

Sometimes the best strategy is to abandon strategy altogether and simply move in the general direction of your goal.

Doing something - anything - that has a chance of succeeding is preferable to simply sitting.

"Life moves on. And so should we."

- Spencer Johnson

Nothing lasts forever, so keep your eyes open for approaching changes

"No man ever steps in the same river twice, for it's not the same river and he's not the same man." - Heraclitus

In "Who Moved My Cheese," two mice, Sniff and Scurry, stumbled upon a massive pile of cheese at Station C. They didn't take it for granted and continued to search for new cheese even after the stockpile began to dwindle.

Every day, the amount of cheese decreased slowly but steadily. When they realized they were about to run out, they decided to continue on their own and soon discovered another massive cheese at Station N.

On the other hand, two humans named Hem and Haw became complacent, reveling in their cheese-filled **comfort zone** at Station C. They were so focused on the cheese that they didn't notice how it was vanishing one piece at a time, and how some corners of it had even gotten moldy. They were blindsided when they woke up one day to find their cheese gone.

Instead of adapting to the new reality and seeking fresh cheese, they were overcome with fear and despair, returning to Station C repeatedly in the hope that their cheese would magically reappear.

Change is the only constant in life, and those who embrace it and adapt will thrive.

Don't get too comfortable with the status quo, or you might find yourself left without any cheese at all.

Look for change.

Instead of assuming that things will always remain the same, keep an eye out for new opportunities.

This allows you to adapt to change and make the most of your life.

"When you are afraid things are going to get worse if you don't do something, it can prompt you into action. But it is not good when you are afraid that it keeps you from doing anything." - Spencer Johnson

Our fears hold us back, but confronting them is easier than we think

"What you are afraid of is never as bad as what you imagine. The fear you let build up in your mind is worse than the situation that actually exists."
- Spencer Johnson

In Spencer Johnson's parable, the humans are stuck in their comfort zone even after running out of cheese. But one of them, Haw, takes the brave step of venturing out to look for new cheese, and his situation improves greatly once he starts moving.

Don't let fear hold you back from progress. Once you find the courage to move on, the grip of fear will weaken.

Your worries about the future may be worse than the reality of change, but standing still will surely lead to disappointment.

"By changing nothing, nothing changes."
- Tony Robbins

Haw eventually finds a new station filled with cheese, but he doesn't stop there. He keeps exploring and searching for new opportunities, knowing that nothing lasts forever.

Life is full of uncertainty, but there's always more "cheese" out there to discover, even if we don't know where or in what form it will appear.

Overcome your fear.

In any situation, taking the first step is the most difficult. But once you get started, everything will improve.

Maintain your focus and keep moving forward.

"A ship is safe in harbor, but that's not what ships are built for." - John A. Shedd

Fixed mindsets hold us back and can make life mediocre

"Life isn't about finding yourself. Life is about creating yourself." - George Bernard Shaw

Science has shown that personality is not set in stone, and yet many of us hold onto the belief that we're stuck with the personality we're born with. This myth keeps us from growing and becoming the best versions of ourselves.

There are five personality myths that hinder our ability to change:

- We can be neatly categorized into personality "types."
- Our personalities are fixed and unchangeable.
- Our past experiences determine our personalities.
- Our personalities must be "discovered" rather than developed.
- Personality tests accurately describe who we are.

But these myths are simply not true. Personality tests that classify people into types oversimplify the complexities of human nature.

Research has shown that our personalities can change dramatically over time, and that past traumas, environment, and our subconscious play a significant role in shaping who we are.

So why not view ourselves as evolving and changing like historical events? When we cling too tightly to the idea of being "true to ourselves," we limit our ability to adapt and grow.

Don't limit yourself to a 'type'.

Don't let predefined personality types rule your life or dictate how you interact with others.

Different people and situations will bring out different aspects of your personality. That is a good thing!

We can change our identities by setting goals

Have you ever considered how our goals shape our identities? Every action we take serves a purpose, and the term "goal" is just another word for purpose.

"Your life does not get better by chance; it gets better by change" - Jim Rohn

Our decisions and actions are all driven by our goals. That's why it's crucial to understand the key components to changing your personality: **exposure, desire, and confidence.**

Firstly, we need to open our eyes to the world and expose ourselves to new experiences and possibilities. As Benjamin Hardy put it, "You can't make decisions and choices if you don't know they exist."

Next, we must focus on our desires and set a goal to strive towards. If our current desires aren't healthy or fulfilling, we can work actively to change them.

Lastly, we must be confident in our ability to achieve our objectives, or we'll never even consider them.

If we want to break free from our limitations and gain the courage to succeed, we must step out of our comfort zone and be willing to embrace failure.

Adopt a growth mindset.

Find the strength to continue pushing yourself to seek new experiences and opportunities. You don't want to be the same person you are today in ten years; instead, embark on a journey of lifelong learning and growth.

"The only thing 'special' about those who transform themselves and their lives is their view of their own future. They refuse to be defined by the past, they see something different and more meaningful, and they never stop fueling that vision." - Benjamin Hardy

By improving the way we view our personalities, we can change our futures

Meet Nate, a young man who, like many of his family members, had always struggled with his weight. But when Nate saw the health problems his parents were facing due to their weight, he knew he needed to make a change.

Nate asked himself some critical questions: "What will my future be like if I continue to struggle with my weight? What will I be like when I'm seventy?" These questions can be tough to answer, but they helped Nate connect with his future self and gain perspective on his current situation.

To identify the future we want, there are four steps to follow.

First, you need to examine the future you've unconsciously resigned yourself to. Consider what your life will be like at the age of seventy. Are you happy with how things turned out? Write your own biography as if you've already lived your entire life.

Next, visualize your future self-three years from now. Imagine what your typical day looks like, how your job is going, and what makes you different from who you are today.

Then, write about these visualizations while freewriting, asking yourself questions such as "What were the major events in my life?" and "What were my most notable achievements?"

Finally, start telling your new story to others and yourself as if it were already true. This helps you believe in your vision and take steps to make it a reality. Just like Nate, you too can adopt a growth mentality and transform your life.

"Change is hard at first, messy in the middle and gorgeous at the end."
- Robin Sharma

Start freewriting about your future.

Only by getting your thoughts down on paper will you begin to realize what you truly desire. Make time for yourself to reflect on who you are. what you stand for, and what you still want to achieve.

Real-world finance is not taught in schools

Our school system is outdated, designed for a time when farming was the norm, and financial education was not a priority. To be financially successful in today's world, it's essential to have a solid understanding of how money and assets work.

One of the most crucial things that we're not taught in school is the difference between an asset and a liability.

The wealthy know the importance of investing in assets that earn money while they sleep, unlike liabilities, which cost money and provide little or no return.

Another critical piece of knowledge missing from our education system is the usefulness of corporations. The wealthy take advantage of corporations to minimize taxes and limit their exposure to risk.

Money is not real; it's an illusion that relies on trust.

The wealthy understand this and know how to manipulate it to their advantage. They buy and sell houses at a profit without ever exchanging actual money.

Once you grasp the basics, financial success comes down to hard work, spotting opportunities, and dedicating yourself to becoming as wealthy as you legally can. It's time to break free from the old-school mentality and take control of your finances to build a better future for yourself.

Pay yourself first each month.

"The poor and the middle-class work for money. The rich have money work for them." - Robert T. Kiyosaki

Let's talk about investing! While it may seem like a daunting task, investing a small portion of your salary each month can be a smart move towards securing your financial future.

Think of it this way: before you even start thinking about paying rent and bills, take a little chunk out of your paycheck and invest it in some medium-to-high risk stocks or bonds. By doing so, you open yourself up to the potential of reaping some major rewards.

Of course, investing always carries a certain degree of risk. That's why it's crucial to only invest what you can afford to lose. With a bit of research and a willingness to take a calculated gamble, you just might find yourself on the path to financial success. So why not give it a try? The potential payoff might just be worth it!

Experience is a more efficient teacher than formal education

"The illiterate of the 21st century will not be those who cannot read and write, but those who cannot learn, unlearn, and relearn." - Alvin Toffler

In today's ever-evolving world, it's more important than ever for entrepreneurs to keep up with the latest developments and continuously refine their skills.

What we learned in school may not be applicable in the current landscape, so it's important to take a critical look and consider new approaches.

One of the best ways to learn is by observing others, both successful and unsuccessful, and then trying things out for yourself.

To achieve financial independence, you must train yourself to see what others overlook and seize opportunities when they arise.

Don't be afraid of failure. It's often the best teacher, and those who are most successful embrace it. Edison and Bell tried countless prototypes before perfecting their inventions, and successful writers have faced numerous rejections before finding success.

While traditional education methods still have value, it's up to you to choose what you need to learn and how to apply that knowledge.

The wealthy tend to be knowledgeable in a wide range of areas, but they hire experts for the details.

Learn what you need to learn.

"If you want a new idea, read an old book" - Ivan Pavlov

Keep filling in gaps in your knowledge and skills by reading books, staying informed about the news, and seeking advice from friends.

As you gain more expertise, you'll begin to spot investment opportunities and put your newfound knowledge into practice. So, take action, keep learning, and seize the opportunities that come your way!

Most people are controlled by two conflicting emotions: fear and greed

"When emotion goes up, intelligence goes down." - Robert Kiyosaki

In the movie Jerry Maguire, when the protagonist gets fired, he takes a bold step and asks the whole company to join him. Although one woman raises her hand, she declines because she's due for a promotion. This reluctance to leave the safety of a comfortable situation is something that many of us can relate to.

But financial independence requires us to step outside of our comfort zones and take risks. We can't just keep running in the rat race and accumulating more liabilities. It's up to us to make a choice and take action.

Our financial behavior is deeply ingrained, influenced by the advice of our parents and the norms of society. We believe that we have to work for someone else and pay taxes, but this belief limits us.

The fear of rejection can be paralyzing, but we need to master it to achieve success.

The desire for wealth can be outweighed by the fear of losing the illusion of financial security, resulting in a conflict between greed and fear.

Successful people take risks and work on controlling their thoughts and emotions.

We can choose to break free from our ancestral instincts and decide for ourselves.

By taking a long-term view and writing down our financial fears, we can begin to overcome them and move forward towards financial independence.

When planning for the long-term, it's key to factor in the likelihood that your preferences will change

Compounding is the magic that turns small efforts into big rewards, but it takes time and consistency. Whether it's building wealth, pursuing a career, or nurturing relationships, the benefits of compounding are enormous.

The problem is, our innate tendency to change and evolve makes it difficult to stick to our long-term plans. We tend to underestimate how much we'll change in the future and assume that our current goals and desires will stay the same.

To make long-term plans that stick, we need to plan with flexibility and moderation in mind. Extreme plans that require us to work tirelessly or sacrifice everything else in our lives are unlikely to last. We must find a balance that allows us to make progress while still enjoying our lives.

When we stick to our plans, we create a compounding effect that can produce incredible results. Just like compound interest, the benefits of our efforts start small but grow over time.

So, take a step back, evaluate your plan, and ensure it's flexible enough to accommodate the changes that life inevitably brings. With persistence and patience, you can achieve anything you set your mind to.

"Aiming, at every point in your working life, to have moderate annual savings, moderate free time, no more than a moderate commute, and at least moderate time with your family, increases the odds of being able to stick with a plan." - Morgan Housel

Consumerism blinds us to what money can buy

In our society, it's easy to fall into the trap of believing that our status and material possessions determine our happiness. But this couldn't be further from the truth.

Research has shown that having a sense of control over our lives is the most reliable predictor of psychological wellbeing. And when it comes to control, money can be a powerful tool.

As financial expert Morgan Housel puts it, money's greatest intrinsic value is its ability to give us control over our time. Instead of spending our money on expensive things, we should consider using it to buy time and control.

Controlling our spending can allow us to choose jobs with more flexible schedules and better work-life balance. To avoid lifestyle inflation, where our spending increases along with our income, it's important to track our expenses and prioritize our spending based on what truly matters.

"Never spend money before you have it." - Thomas Jefferson

But what do we do with the extra time and control we gain from being mindful with our money? According to gerontologist Karl Pillemer, the key to a fulfilling life is not in earning more money or acquiring more possessions, but in cultivating quality friendships, a sense of purpose, and strong personal relationships.

By tracking our expenses and prioritizing our spending based on what truly matters, we can achieve a sense of control over our lives and ultimately lead happier, more fulfilling lives.

"We work jobs we hate, to buy things we don't need, to impress people we don't like." - Tyler Durden

To stay healthy, we have to eat well and keep moving

"Essential to happiness in life are something to do, something to love, and something to hope for." - Hector Garcia

Who said getting fit and healthy had to be a chore? According to the Okinawans, simple and consistent movements throughout the day are key to longevity.

So, put down those running shoes and forget about joining the local sports team. A walk around the neighborhood, some time spent in the garden, or even a few arm movements can do wonders for your health.

Of course, exercise is only half the equation. Okinawans also emphasize the importance of a healthy diet, full of fresh vegetables and homemade meals shared with loved ones.

And if you're looking to shed a few pounds, consider the Japanese philosophy of 'hara hachi bu' - minimal eating for maximum benefit. Fill your plate with a variety of colorful fruits and vegetables, and take the time to savor each bite.

Don't forget to take small exercise breaks throughout the day - set a reminder on your phone or challenge your friends to a weekly step count competition. It's time to embrace a simpler, healthier way of life.

"A fit body, a calm mind, a house full of love. These things cannot be bought – they must be earned." - Naval Ravikant

PART 3: LOVE AND CONNECTION

We can't connect to others if we are disconnected from ourselves

In today's fast-paced world, distractions are everywhere. From our demanding work schedules to the constant barrage of media and technology, it's easy to get caught up in the hustle and bustle.

Despite our many connections, many of us feel lonely and anxious. Our phones and social media may seem like they help us stay in touch, but they also provide a convenient escape from confronting our thoughts and feelings.

The key to connecting with others lies within ourselves. **To truly understand others, we must first learn to listen to and understand ourselves.**

Mindfulness can help us recognize and accept our negative emotions, instead of being overwhelmed by them. Instead of seeking comfort in our work, social media, or relationships, we must find peace within ourselves.

"It is so important to come home to ourselves and cease being the victims of our own circumstances." - Thich Nhat Hanh

By becoming at peace with who we are, approaching our emotions with curiosity instead of judgment, and learning to build meaningful relationships, we can help those around us and live a fulfilling life.

"When we come back to ourselves...and take refuge in our inner island, we become a home for ourselves and a refuge for others at the same time."
- Thich Nhat Hanh

Take a break from social media.

Take a break if you use social media to avoid unpleasant thoughts or feelings.

Delete the apps over the weekend, or temporarily deactivate your account.

"The nearer a man comes to a calm mind, the closer he is to strength."
- Marcus Aurelius

Reconnecting with our bodies grounds us in the present moment

Our modern way of life contributes significantly to a disconnect between our minds and bodies. We are physically present while sitting in our offices or working on our laptops, but our minds wander.

We spend so much time ruminating on the past or worrying about the future that we forget to appreciate the beauty of the present moment.

"I shouldn't immerse myself so completely in work that I get drowned in it. I should have time to live, to get in touch with the refreshing and healing elements that are in me and around me." - Thich Nhat Hanh

The best way to ground ourselves in the present moment is to learn how to become aware of our bodies through meditation.

Paying attention to our posture, breathing mindfully, and scanning our bodies without judgement for discomfort helps to bring our minds back to where we are physically and gives us a sense of calm.

Being in the present moment allows us to be more resilient during difficult times.

"The best way of taking care of the future is to take care of the present, because the future is made of the present." - Thich Nhat Hanh

When we can appreciate the beauty around us, as well as all of the wonderful and complex tasks our bodies perform in each moment, we can begin to put our daily problems into perspective.

When our minds and bodies are at ease in the present, the past and future can no longer overwhelm us.

Ground yourself in your breath.

Close your eyes and focus on your breathing when you're feeling overwhelmed. As you inhale and exhale, try counting or repeating positive mantras.

Mindful meditation helps us build compassion for ourselves and others.

Mindfulness does not imply mastering difficult yoga postures or sitting silently for long periods of time. Meditation is not meant to be difficult, and there are numerous ways to incorporate it into our daily lives.

We can start doing breathing exercises between stressful meetings or phone calls, or we can learn to walk mindfully and incorporate it into our daily commute.

"We can live our daily life seeing everything in the light of interbeing. Then we will not be caught in our small self. We will see our connection, our joy, and our suffering everywhere."
- Thich Nhat Hanh

When we begin to see ourselves as interconnected with the rest of the world, our problems become less significant in comparison to those of others.

Recognizing that we are a part of the Earth allows us to share in its beauty as well as its suffering. Mindfulness helps us connect with others while also developing compassion for ourselves.

Meditative practice on a daily basis improves our empathy and resilience. We begin to heal from past trauma and find joy in the present as we become more at ease with our own bodies and practice compassion for our minds.

Add mindfulness practices to your daily routine.

No matter how hectic your schedule is, try to incorporate meditation into your daily routine.

Mindful walking, mindful eating, and breathing exercises can help you relax your body and reduce workplace stress.

If you want your love to grow and flourish, nourish it with happiness and share it with others

Consider adding a teaspoon of salt to your glass of water. It would be nearly impossible to drink.

And consider throwing that spoonful of salt into a river. It won't make much of a difference.

Similarly, if our hearts are small and closed, we are easily upset by the mistakes and flaws of others. However, if we open our hearts, we will discover empathy and compassion for our fellow humans.

It's as simple as that: love requires nourishment. Happiness is the source of that nourishment.

Only when you are content can you truly open your heart and love others.

Understanding someone's suffering is the best gift you can give another person. Understanding is love's other name. If you don't understand, you can't love." - Thich Nhat Hanh

Zen Buddhism teaches us about happiness and how to achieve it. We sometimes believe that happiness will come to us through materialistic desires. True happiness, on the other hand, is the result of mindfulness.

Walking is a quick exercise that can help you experience happiness through mindfulness. Instead of focusing on the destination and rushing, consider the movement of your body and the beauty of your surroundings.

When you practice mindfulness, you will notice beauty in the simplest of things, such as a flower in bloom.

Pay attention to your surroundings and your body, as well as your movement. Take everything in. That is how you will find true happiness. When you find happiness in the present moment, you can share it with others and help them find happiness as well.

Love is made up of joy, equanimity, compassion, and loving-kindness

Love is about much more than finding an attractive and successful mate.

To understand love, you must first understand its four main characteristics: **joy, equanimity, and compassion and loving-kindness.**

Joy is all about experiencing deep and lasting happiness. When we are filled with joy, we want to share it with others.

Equanimity is also referred to as inclusiveness. This trait entails the ability to blur the lines between yourself and another person so that their suffering becomes your suffering.

Compassion enables us to see and comprehend suffering. This improves our ability to listen and empathize.

Loving-kindness is the practice of using mindfulness to make others happy. This characteristic enables us to bring joy to even the most depressed heart.

True love is not about acquiring something, but rather about being able to recognize and comprehend another person's pain.

Be generous.

When you're happy, share it with others.

Allow your light to shine on others so that they can be happier as well.

"The art of happiness is also the art of suffering well. When we learn to acknowledge, embrace, and understand our suffering, we suffer much less... There is no place where there is only happiness and no suffering." - Thich Nhat Hanh

Mindful love and connection heal our hearts

Unleash the Power of Mindful Love!

Have you ever stopped to think about the word "love"? It's a word that we often use so casually, from "I love ice cream" to "I love my friends". But true love is so much more than just a word.

By being mindful of our use of "love", we can restore its true significance. **Mindful love is all-encompassing, embracing the good and the bad in a person, without judgment.**

Imagine the impact we could have if we suspended our tendencies to judge and reject, and instead, become healers. The ancient Sanskrit word for compassion, **karuna**, embodies this idea. It goes beyond empathy and means to do everything in our power to alleviate another's suffering.

Think of it like medicine. When you go to the doctor, you don't just want them to understand your pain, you want them to do something about it, to heal you. Love is similar in this way. It not only helps us understand someone's pain, but gives us the power to heal them.

But here's the thing, love is a two-way street. It takes effort and compassion from both sides to truly heal and bring happiness to each other's lives. Embrace the power of mindful love today!

Partners must be healers.

This means that if you are in pain, you must sometimes seek assistance. This can be difficult, but asking your partner for help is the only way to achieve mutual healing.

PART 4: PHILOSOPHY

Finding Simplicity and Peace in Life through Cultivating Wisdom and Living in Harmony with Nature

Our ability to think rationally distinguishes us from all other creatures in the universe. But rational wisdom does not come naturally to us; we must work hard to exercise and develop this ability.

Wisdom enables us to comprehend nature, both our own and that of the world around us. And understanding the world allows us to live in harmony with it rather than stressing ourselves out over things we cannot control.

Many people spend their lives pursuing wealth or status. However, disaster or hardship can strike anyone at any time, and it is pointless to complain that the world is unfair. **We can enjoy the good things in life, but only with the knowledge that they can all be taken away from us** - and they will, one day.

"If you live in harmony with nature you will never be poor; if you live according what others think, you will never be rich." - Seneca

If you learn to live simply, and even practice living as if you were poor on occasion, you will be able to live secure in the knowledge that even if you lose everything, you will be at peace.

Only by mentally preparing for the worst-case scenario, including death, can we truly achieve peace.

"It is not the man who has too little that is poor, but the one who hankers after more." - Seneca

Simplify your life.

Are there any material goods or pleasures in your life that you don't think you need?

Is there anywhere you could cut back? Living with less will enrich your life and reduce your stress.

The single most valuable thing you have is your mind

Embark on a Journey to Inner Peace with Your Mind as Your Compass.

When life gets rough and stormy, it's easy to feel lost and helpless. But there's one thing that always stays within our grasp - our thoughts and mentality.

A peaceful mind is like a sturdy ship, equipped to weather any storm that comes its way.

With a tranquil mindset, you'll be able to tackle challenges head-on, handle success with grace, and make firm decisions with ease. But when your thoughts are cluttered, you'll never find the calmness you seek.

Your mind is not just your own, but it's your permanent abode. **No matter where you go, if your mind is troubled, you won't be able to escape the chaos.**

That's where philosophy comes in. It helps us delve inward and cultivate a sound mind.

Instead of just skimming through multiple authors, choose a few that resonate with you and delve deep into their teachings. Apply what you learn to your life and see the transformation for yourself.

Make time for quiet contemplation and never stop learning. One new thing a day keeps the anxiety away!

"The primary indication, to my thinking, of a well-ordered mind is a man's ability to remain in one place and linger in his own company." - Seneca

Be happy in tranquility.

Being wealthy or well-traveled will not make you happy in the long run. **Create inner peace and cultivate your mind so that you are always pleasant company for yourself.**

Do not expect others to fill a void in your life, but cultivate friendship with loyal and virtuous people

A calm mind allows you to surround yourself with true friends, which is one of the many ways it helps you build a good life.

Many people associate with those from whom they hope to gain something, such as flattery, wealth, or status. **Those who cultivate inner wisdom, on the other hand, have no need to seek these things from others.**

"Withdraw into yourself, as far as you can. Associate with those who will make a better man of you. Welcome those whom you yourself can improve. The process is mutual; for men learn while they teach." - Seneca

By learning to enjoy your own company and fostering a sense of abundance and giving, you too can become a true friend to those in your life.

But choose wisely, as the people you surround yourself with can greatly impact your growth and well-being.

Friends should inspire each other to strive for constant improvement and not just reflect each other's flaws.

Trust is a crucial foundation of any relationship, but don't give it away freely. When you do find a true friend, cherish them and trust them fully.

Remember, it's better to have a few genuine friends than many shallow acquaintances, and having no friends is better than having fair-weather friends.

So, take control of your relationships and cultivate inner wisdom to build a fulfilling life.

Choose your friends carefully.

If any of your relationships feel unhealthy and are causing you more harm than good, it's time to let them go. Surround yourself with people you enjoy being with!

"Waste no more time arguing about what a good man should be. Be one."
- Marcus Aureilius

Know what you can control and what you can't

Do you feel trapped within the walls of your own mind, with worries, fears, and doubts taking over your thoughts and hindering your mental freedom? You're not alone.

But it's time to break free from that prison. The only thing we have complete control over is ourselves, and it's time to take that power back. Don't let anxieties and uncertainties steer you away from your own liberation.

Epictetus, a famous Stoic philosopher, knew all too well the feeling of being captive in circumstances beyond his control. He was a slave, but his wisdom was free.

"Uneducated people blame other people when they are doing badly, those whose education is underway blame themselves, but a fully educated person blames no one." - Epictetus

We often feel imprisoned by our desires for things we don't have, fear of things we don't understand, and people or situations that control us.

But it's time to let go of those negative emotions and focus on what is truly within our power - ourselves.

True peace can be found in the humblest of circumstances when we rely on ourselves and don't seek the approval of others or the abundance of material possessions.

Stoicism, predating Christianity, is based on logic and the belief that **"nothing happens... without a predetermined cause."** This means that even our successes and failures are predetermined, and it's crucial to understand that we have less control than we think.

The idea of predeterminism is not about blaming anyone for their circumstances, but about acknowledging that external suffering is beyond our control. So, let go of that weight, focus on yourself, and find peace in knowing that the only thing that truly matters is the present moment.

Accept what you can't change.

Master your mind: it is your only true possession

Let's face it, our fears and insecurities can hold us back from discovering our true potential and living life to the fullest. But, according to **Epictetus**, confronting these feelings and understanding the root of our disturbances is key to living an effective life.

Stoicism teaches us to embrace adversity and flourish even in the toughest of circumstances.

Epictetus invites us to view life as a gift, with each moment being a part of a larger, meaningful journey. The way we perceive our current situation shapes our lives and **it's up to us to choose what we focus on.**

Despite being a slave, Epictetus found peace by adopting a humble perspective and learning to live freely within it. To achieve inner freedom, one must put in the hard work and dedication necessary to reach their goals.

Take your mind and your life seriously and unleash your true potential through hard work and self-discovery. The key to mental liberation lies within you.

"What Epictetus insists we should do, in order to live as effectively as possible, is confront our impressions, especially those that disturb us." - Anthony Long

Don't think too highly of material objects.

According to Epictetus, no physical item, including your own body, is ever truly yours.

Material possessions break or fade; don't let them have a strong influence on your mental state.

Live by dedicating yourself to truth, freeing yourself of influence, and seeking reason inwardly

Don't waste your time and energy trying to impress others with your work or social connections. To truly be yourself, focus on your unwavering quest for truth, free from the opinions and feelings of others.

By taking the search for truth seriously, any external distractions will become irrelevant.

A fundamental part of living in harmony with your existence is avoiding the accumulation of wealth or indulging in excess. Money, a byproduct of desire, holds no importance in Stoic philosophy.

The truth, as Epictetus notes, is often far from the pursuit of wealth and success in business, where deceit and dishonesty are often rationalized.

"We do tell lies, while we are ready to advance the proofs that we shouldn't."
- Epictetus

Preconceived ideas and beliefs can lead us to create a false narrative in our minds, and our judgement is often clouded by these incomplete stories.

Lies and misinformation lead to a vicious cycle of confusion and it becomes difficult for us and others to determine what's true.

When making decisions, only draw conclusions when you're absolutely certain of the validity of the information you're using as the basis for your judgement.

Your thoughts should be grounded in truth, without a shadow of doubt.

Cultivate silence.

The majority of daily conversations are about trivial matters. A Stoic mind prefers silence to meaningless banter.

"Don't try to be funny, it's a behavior that easily lapses into vulgarity." - Epictetus

PART 5: HUMAN PSYCHOLOGY

Your past doesn't determine your future

"Don't let yourself controlled by three things: people, money, or past experience." - Unknown

Let's dive into the fascinating world of psychology and explore the opposing views of Sigmund Freud and Alfred Adler on the impact of childhood experiences on our lives.

Freud believed that our self-image is deeply rooted in our psyche from an early age, and negative experiences can lead to ongoing struggles throughout our lives. He suggested that we spend much of our adult life trying to overcome the limiting beliefs and trauma of our past.

On the other hand, Adler saw things differently. While he acknowledged that our style of life is formed early on, he didn't believe it was a fixed point of our character. He argued that we can change who we are at any given moment.

But here's the catch: even if you can trace all your flaws back to a few instances in your childhood, you won't be able to change them in the present unless you believe that something different can happen.

You have the power to choose a new outlook and break free from old patterns at any time.

Take control of your own destiny.

The key to your own happiness lies within yourself and not in the hands of others.

By prioritizing yourself and living in the present moment, you can experience a positive transformation in your life.

Remember that you can only alter the present, but that power to make a difference is entirely yours.

"Everyone thinks of changing the world but no one thinks of changing himself."
- Leo Tolstoy

Our behaviors are governed by two systems of thinking

Why do we trust some people intuitively more than others when there is no prior basis for that trust? What **unconscious biases** influence our worldviews and assumptions?

"Nothing in life is as important as you think it is, while you are thinking about it." - Daniel Kahneman

Daniel Kahneman, a Nobel Prize-winning economist and psychologist, unravel the mysteries of the human mind as he explores the **dual processes of thinking** in his book "Thinking, Fast and Slow". Kahneman provides a captivating insight into decision-making, uncertainty, and behavioral economics.

As explained by Daniel Kahneman, **System 1** is your fast thinking, intuitive, automatic and emotional self - quickly determining distances and processing impressions.

On the other hand, **System 2** is your slow thinking, deliberate, analytical and reason-driven self, helping you find solutions to complex problems.

Intuition is the foundation of our decisions, created by the memory function in our mind that builds up over time. System 1 takes this intuition and forms patterns, while System 2 makes sense of these patterns.
The two systems work together to make our choices and judgments, with System 1 providing the foundation and System 2 adding order and logic.

Although System 1 is prone to cognitive biases, it has played an important role in our evolutionary history, helping us make quick decisions in life-threatening situations. Don't underestimate the power of your intuition, as System 1 is the secret author of many of your choices.

As Kahneman says, "Expert intuition strikes us as magical, but it is not. Each of us performs feats of intuitive expertise many times each day." Embrace the magic of your mind and discover the hidden depths of your cognitive systems.

"System 2 believes itself to be where the action is, but system 1 is the secret author of many of the choices and judgements you make." - Daniel Kahneman

Our beliefs are structured by memory and narrative sense-making

"The confidence that individuals have in their beliefs depends mostly on the quality of the story they can tell about what they see, even if they see little."

- Daniel Kahneman

System 1 is fast and intuitive, relying on quick perception and recognition to form patterns and make decisions. On the other hand, System 2 is more deliberate and analytical, only activated when necessary for focused problem-solving.

By understanding these systems in others and ourselves, we can recognize the unconscious biases and assumptions that govern our thinking. **Confirmation bias and the halo effect** are just a few examples of how our quick, emotional response can shape our beliefs and decisions.

However, **our brains are always looking to save energy and make decisions as quickly as possible, even if it means risking a wrong call**. This can lead to our brains perceiving problems as simpler than they actually are, and system 1 taking charge when it's not equipped to handle the situation. On the flip side, using system 2 requires more effort and can leave us feeling mentally drained.

Don't let emotion navigate your decisions.

Emotions can easily cloud your judgement, but you must not allow them to. Examine situations objectively.

Weigh the benefits and drawbacks, then use your reasoning to make the best decision for you. This is especially true when it comes to money.

"Changing one's mind about human nature is hard work, and changing one's mind for the worse about oneself is even harder." - Daniel Kahneman

Our two systems of thought produce two entwined selves

"The only test of rationality is not whether a person's beliefs and preferences are reasonable, but whether they are internally consistent."

- Daniel Kahneman

According to Daniel Kahneman, each of us is governed by two distinct 'selves'.

The remembering self, which is aligned with system 1, shapes and selects the memories from which the experiencing self draws.

The experiencing self, on the other hand, is aligned with system 2 and evaluates present and past information to make a decision.

Think of it this way, the remembering self-curates the memories that shape our understanding of the world, while the experiencing self-evaluates information to make informed decisions. But beware, the remembering self's recollection may not always be accurate, and relying solely on the past can lead to flawed thinking.

Kahneman stresses that rational thinking demands a balance of informed intuition and reason, guided by logic and evidence.

Our intuition works to simplify our world by connecting emotions, events, and outcomes, which eventually form our identity and determine our responses. This is what Kahneman calls the **"affect heuristic"**, where our emotions play a big role in decision-making, making life easier for our minds.

However, knowing facts and statistics about human behavior does not guarantee a shift in our understanding or beliefs. As Kahneman says, "**The only test of rationality is not whether a person's beliefs and preferences are reasonable, but whether they are internally consistent**."

So, it's up to us to question our preconceived ideas and let logic and reason guide us towards rational thinking.

"Even compelling causal statistics will not change long-held beliefs or beliefs rooted in personal experience."

- Daniel Kahneman

Stay open to new ideas.

Social pressures can work against us

"We all fool ourselves from time to time in order to keep our thoughts and beliefs consistent with what we have already done or decided" - Robert Cialdini

Have you ever left a restaurant feeling a little more satisfied after being given a piece of chocolate for free with your bill? These gestures might seem like acts of kindness, but they're actually playing by the rule of reciprocation.

When someone does us a favor or gifts us something, it's human nature to feel obligated to return the favor to avoid the guilt of not doing so. We also have a social responsibility to repay kindness, as those who don't can be perceived as taking advantage of others.

Our ancestors shared food and tools knowing that they would receive something in return. Today, businesses use the rule of reciprocation to their advantage, but it's not just about receiving, it's about being seen as good and honest.

This is where the consistency principle comes in. When we make a commitment, we follow through, even if it puts us or our reputation in danger, because we want to align our actions with our words.

Have you ever been approached by a salesperson who's convinced you to make a small purchase? This is known as the 'foot-in-the-door' technique and it's a sneaky way to exploit the principle of consistency.

A small initial purchase establishes a person as a customer, making them more likely to commit to spending more money in the future.

"Our best evidence of what people truly feel and believe comes less from their words than from their deeds." - Robert Cialdini

Think before you reciprocate.

Although it is appropriate to return genuine favors, always think twice before doing so in a business setting.

Do you really want that gym membership, or are you just getting it as a freebie from the gym?

Because we hate to miss out on opportunities, scarcity makes us act

"People seem to be more motivated by the thought of losing something than by the thought of gaining something of equal value." - Robert Cialdini

Humans despise missing out, which is why we are much more likely to purchase something if it is only available for a limited time. we perceive limited items to be more valuable. This is the scarcity principle at work.

Businesses use **scarcity** to increase sales through limited-time promotions and sales.

In one 1982 study, people purchased three times as much when told it was part of a limited-time sale as they would if there was no limit. Shoppers also purchased six times more meat when told that they were the only ones who knew about the sale - the limited availability of the sale, combined with the limited knowledge, drove them to buy more.

Scarcity is most powerful when availability has recently and unexpectedly decreased and there is competition for the available items. This is why people pay more at auctions when they know others are bidding.

When you go to buy something because it's on sale for a limited time or you're told there are only a few left, consider whether you really want it or if you're being duped.

We are more likely to do things if we see others doing them, just as competition makes us want something more because it is socially desirable. This is the social proof principle at work.

We are more likely to laugh at a bad joke if others are laughing, and we are more likely to donate to charity if there are coins in the bucket already.

Companies use this principle to promote products by saying they are 'best-sellers.

When we understand the tools that people use to manipulate us, we can take a step back when we see them being used against us.

We are more likely to comply with authority figures and people we like

Would you buy a product from a stranger on the street? Probably not. But what if it's your friend who's starting a business? Chances are, you'll give it a try.

This is the **likability** principle in action. Our innate preference for likeable people is easily exploitable, especially by salespeople who know how to flatter and make themselves relatable to us.

But it's not just our friends who can influence us. Our perception of someone's appearance also matters. **We tend to assume that good-looking people are friendly and smart, even if it's a flawed assumption.**

On the other hand, the principle of **authority** is equally powerful. From early childhood, we look to authority figures for guidance and direction, often without questioning their motives. This can lead us to blindly follow their commands, even if we don't like them.

However, it's important to remember that not all authority figures have our best interests at heart.

Before following their instructions, take a moment to reflect and ensure that their requests align with our values and beliefs. After all, we are the masters of our own destiny.

"The world abounds with cults populated by dependent people who are led by a charismatic figure." - Robert Cialdini

Look out for wily salespeople.

If you want to buy something, be aware of who is selling it to you. Are they being overly nice, flattering, or relatable despite the fact that they don't know you?

If this is the case, they are most likely attempting to manipulate you.

We often favor feeling right over being right

Looking to express our individuality and make our mark in the world, we often let our beliefs and opinions define who we are. But have you ever stopped to ask yourself **why you hold the opinions you do?**

It's easy to spot emotional bias in others, but when it comes to our own views, we might not be so aware. How we process information and arrive at our beliefs is influenced by different modes of thinking.

In 'preacher' mode, we spread the word and defend our position passionately.

In 'prosecutor' mode, we attack opposing beliefs and pick them apart.

In 'politician' mode, popularity trumps accuracy, while in 'scientist' mode, we question everything, seeking evidence and being open to revising our beliefs in light of new data.

A recent study of start-up founders is a prime example of the power of adopting a scientific approach. Those who received entrepreneurship training that emphasized **scientific thinking** earned 40 times more than those who received conventional business training after just one year!

Even the most innovative businesses and leaders can be held back by clinging to outdated beliefs. Just think of BlackBerry's founder, Mike Lazaridis, who refused to embrace the touch-screen iPhone and stuck with physical keyboards, or Steve Jobs, who initially dismissed the idea of putting a computer in a phone. In both cases, they would have been better served by questioning their assumptions and being open to change.

Think more like a scientist.

Practice valuing data over assumptions and truth over popular opinion.

Let people know it's okay to challenge received wisdom. Create a culture of questioning at work and at home. Encourage others to question their own beliefs.

"You must unlearn what you have learned." - Yoda

Confident humility is the doorway to wisdom and success

In a world where certainty is praised and praised as a symbol of power, it's easy to forget that true strength lies in being open to new perspectives.

"Being wrong is the only way I feel sure I've learned anything" - Daniel Kahneman

From brilliant scientists and artists to great leaders and presidents, the common denominator of success is their ability to embrace cognitive flexibility and consider every angle before making a decision.

"Progress is impossible without change, and those who cannot change their minds cannot change anything." This quote by George Bernard Shaw perfectly captures the importance of being able to adapt to new ideas.

In fact, Good Judgment Project's regular forecasting tournaments have shown that those who are willing to revise their forecasts regularly are more likely to make accurate predictions.

Franklin D. Roosevelt, the President of the United States, was a firm believer in the power of experimentation and wasn't afraid to experiment with bold, persistent change.

He trusted that the public would follow his lead, and that trust led to his election as President four times.

Sometimes, emphasizing what will not change is the most effective way to persuade people to embrace change.

Define yourself by your values rather than your opinions.

Examine what really matters to you, then appraise your opinions accordingly.

Invite people to question your thinking.

Set up a 'challenge network' of supportive friends who can pressure-test your views.

We should all welcome being proved wrong

"A hallmark of wisdom is knowing when it's time to abandon some of your most treasured tools - and some of the most cherished parts of your identity."
- Adam Grant

Empower yourself with the power of knowledge and wisdom, for the **road to progress begins with accepting what we don't know**.

Each new invention starts with a daring hypothesis, one that may challenge conventional wisdom. From the invention of the printing press to the launch of the space program, great discoveries and advancements wouldn't have happened if we always demanded proof before taking the leap.

By learning to distinguish between beliefs and facts, we open ourselves to new and exciting discoveries.

However, our own intelligence sometimes hinders our ability to see the world clearly. Research shows that people with higher IQs are more likely to fall into the trap of thinking in stereotypes due to their quick recognition of patterns.

But, with a bit of mental and emotional effort, we can break free from past biases and learned opinions, separating our identity from our beliefs.

Embracing new ideas in both our personal and professional lives is a surefire path to happiness and satisfaction, while sticking rigidly to our plans often leads to missed opportunities and unhappiness.

Regular reappraisals in our relationships can also lead to more positive outcomes, allowing us to objectively assess what's working and what isn't. So, let's embrace the unknown and discover what lies beyond our current perceptions.

Work on your rethinking skills.

Go looking for information that contradicts your views, test it out, and be open to change.

Factor a regular 'life checkup' into your schedule.

Treat your life as you do your health: examine how it's all going, and fix what's not right.

PART 6: FOCUS AND PURPOSE

Task switching breaks focus and decreases productivity

As we move further into the digital age, our ability to stay focused on one idea or task has become increasingly challenging. With an ever-flowing stream of information at our fingertips, our minds are constantly being pulled in different directions.

The myth of multitasking as a productivity booster has been debunked, as switching focus from task to task takes a toll on our mental abilities. In fact, studies have shown that workers switch tasks every three minutes on average, while students switch every 65 seconds!

This constant distraction leads to a decrease in IQ, memory recall, creativity, and even increases the risk of making mistakes.

"If you spend your time switching a lot, then the evidence suggests you will be slower, you'll make more mistakes, you'll be less creative, and you'll remember less of what you do." - Johann Hari

But the consequences of a lack of focus go beyond individual productivity. Distracted driving is a leading cause of death worldwide, and in a functioning democracy, citizens must be able to focus and identify important problems, find solutions, and petition the government to make changes.

It's time to reclaim our focus, to slow down and give our minds the time they need to process information, reflect, and be productive in both our personal and professional lives.

Get into a flow state.

Find a way to immerse yourself in an activity by pursuing a meaningful and challenging goal; it could be as simple as reading a new book or participating in a sport.

Let your mind wander.

A walk in the nature allows your mind to reflect on your experiences, make connections, and consider long-term goals.

Many modern technologies are designed to be distracting

Are you aware of the hidden forces that drive our social media experience? It may come as a surprise, but social media companies have a vested interest in keeping you glued to your screens.

The more time you spend on their platforms, the more money they make from advertisements. Every click, swipe, and message is recorded and analyzed to create a personalized profile that advertisers use to target you with ads. And, have you noticed how every time you log in, you're served with content that keeps you scrolling?

That's because these social media platforms use algorithms designed to keep you hooked. But, it's not just the algorithms that are at play. Many apps and social media sites are built to trigger the satisfying sensation of receiving likes and retweets.

The constant stream of notifications and vibrations only add to the **temptation to switch tasks** and check your devices regularly.

And, here's the twist - we're drawn to negativity on social media. Our brains have an evolutionary bias to look for danger, and as a result, we tend to engage more with negative content.

This leads to a vicious cycle, where algorithms show us more divisive and outrageous content, leading to a polarized online world.

Have you ever noticed how Twitter seems to be awash with angry tweets and Facebook is increasingly recommending extremist groups? Anger not only distorts our attention, but it also puts our nervous systems in fight-or-flight mode, reducing our ability to think critically.

To put an end to the cycle of addiction and negativity on social media, we need to consider alternative business models. A subscription-based or publicly owned social media that functions as a utility could be the answer we're looking for.

"An algorithm that prioritizes keeping you glued to the screen will unintentionally but inevitably-prioritize outraging and angering you. If it's more enraging, it's more engaging." - Johann Hari

Change your app notification settings.

Reduce the number of notifications you receive throughout the day to improve your focus and reduce task switching.

Life is full of stress, but did you know it can seriously impact your ability to focus?

Financial insecurity can create stress and leave you unable to concentrate fully on the task at hand. But, in Finland, a universal basic income helped reduce stress without hindering work.

Long hours of work can lead to exhaustion, lack of productivity, and distractions, but a New Zealand company's switch to a four-day workweek showed an improvement in employee engagement and a decrease in social media distractions.

On the other hand, **sleep deprivation can hamper your focus, memory, and ability to perform** even the simplest tasks. A diet filled with processed foods can rob your brain of the essential nutrients it needs for focus.

But it's not just about what you eat. The air we breathe and the food we eat can be contaminated with pollutants, such as lead and iron from industry and car engines, which shorten our attention spans and affect our brain.

Children are particularly vulnerable to these cognitive delays and attention disorders, as they can be exposed to toxic substances during crucial developmental stages.

Johann Hari said it best: **"If you disrupt your body, by depriving it of the right nutrients or pumping it full of pollutants, your ability to pay attention will also be disrupted."**

The rising global trend of ADHD diagnoses, particularly among children, can be linked to the stress, insecurity, and poor nutrition in our lives. Childhood trauma can also increase the likelihood of ADHD by three times, which highlights the importance of identifying the root cause of a child's inability to focus.

Allow children unstructured playtime.

Spending time outside with other children allows children to develop the creativity and intrinsic motivation required for deep focus throughout their lives.

Being indifferent to death is key to survival

Viktor Frankl, a Holocaust survivor and renowned psychiatrist, philosopher, and writer, explores the depths of the human spirit in his memoir, Man's Search For Meaning. Through his time in Nazi concentration camps, Frankl discovered the power of logotherapy - a method that helps individuals find meaning in their lives, even amidst suffering.

Frankl's teachings, which emerged from his own traumatic experiences, have solidified his legacy as a leader in modern psychology.

After observing the prisoners' reactions to their traumatic experiences, Frankl made a groundbreaking realization that trauma processing has three stages.

Initially, the prisoners were in **shock**, but as they adjusted, they entered a period of **apathy or emotional numbness**. This was followed by a stage of **disillusionment**, which often happened after they had survived and left the camp.

Frankl observed that **prisoners who refused to accept the reality of their situation were the first to die**, whereas those who surrendered to their fate found the strength to endure.

He famously stated, **"Man does not simply exist but always decides what his existence will be, what he will become in the next moment."**

Accepting death as a possibility allowed many detainees to survive the unimaginable horrors of the concentration camps. By surrendering to the present moment and freeing their minds from the fear of the future, prisoners were able to summon the apathy they needed to survive.

Even the most basic necessities of life were taken away from prisoners, but by accepting their reality, they were able to endure and find moments of hope in the darkest of circumstances. Whether it was stealing a pair of shoes from a dead body or hiding in a pile of manure to avoid being led to the gas chambers, apathy gave prisoners the courage to face the unknown.

Frankl's findings teach us that resistance is a complex psychological mechanism, but it often makes us vulnerable to our surroundings.

Embrace the power of acceptance to discover a new perspective on the human experience.

Finding the meaning to your life is your own responsibility

"Everything can be taken from a man but one thing: the last of the human freedoms - to choose one's attitude in any given set of circumstances, to choose one's own way." - Viktor Frankl

When it comes to the game of chess, even the greatest players can't tell you what the one, ultimate move is. Instead, each situation on the board requires a unique solution.

Similarly, life does not have a universal meaning - it's up to each individual to create their own meaning through their choices and actions.

According to psychiatrist and logo therapist Viktor Frankl, meaning can only be found by embracing life's challenges and taking responsibility for our own existence.

Frankl's philosophy encourages us to resist escapism and instead actively search for meaning in everyday life.

He found meaning even in the brutal conditions of the concentration camps by focusing on his love for his wife and clinging to the memory of her.

It's a reminder that we hold the power to determine our own mental state and find meaning, even in the face of pain and suffering. **Don't rely on others to bring comfort - instead, take responsibility for your own mental well-being and find meaning in the moments that matter.**

"When we are no longer able to change a situation, we are challenged to change ourselves." - Viktor Frankl

Facing your fears may make them disappear

"An abnormal reaction to an abnormal situation is normal behavior."
- Viktor Frankl

PART 7: MENTAL HEALTH

Low moods give us the urge to do things that will ultimately keep us down

Sometimes, when we're feeling down, we end up making choices that only make things worse.

We might reach for a drink with friends to try to feel better, but end up feeling worse the next day. Instead, we could choose to hit the gym, which would boost our mood with endorphins and help us feel better overall.

It's not uncommon to feel stuck and unable to make decisions when we're in a bad mood. But it's important to keep making choices, even if they're not perfect. To help guide our decisions, we can think about our personal values, rather than just our emotions in the moment.

To identify our values, we need to ask ourselves what's truly important to us, whether we're living in accordance with those values, and what small changes we could make today to bring us closer to those goals.

Start with one small change that you know you can implement every day. Then make a promise to yourself that you will follow through on it.

Consistency is key when it comes to forming new habits. By starting small and practicing healthy habits regularly, we're more likely to make better choices in the future.

Practice self-compassion.

Rather than kicking yourself when you're down, pay attention to negative self-talk as it arises and think of someone you care about. Consider how you would respond to them if they felt the same way you do, and then apply that same response to yourself.

Imagine all your problems have disappeared.

Make a list of the first signs that your mood issues had resolved. What would you do differently and how would you live?

This assists us in shifting your problem to a solution and moving forward.

"Tools might look great in a box. But they only help when you get them out and start practicing how to use them."
- Dr. Julie Smith

Stress is not our enemy, but a valuable tool

"We cannot untangle stress from a meaningful life. Whatever your unique personal values, anything that you strive towards and work for is going to require your stress response to get you there."
- Dr. Julie Smith

Our brains are like information processing machines, constantly analyzing our surroundings and making decisions about how to respond to different situations. But sometimes we feel overwhelmed or uneasy, and it's all because of cortisol - a hormone that tells our bodies to release energy to help us cope with stress.

The truth is, stress isn't always bad for us. In fact, it can be a powerful motivator that propels us towards our goals. Rather than trying to eliminate stress from our lives, we should learn to harness it and use it to our advantage. As Dr. Julie Smith says, "anything that you strive towards and work for is going to require your stress response to get you there."

Of course, chronic stress can be harmful if we don't take care of ourselves. It's important to recognize the signs of burnout, such as feeling emotionally drained or disconnected from others. Chronic stress can also lead to physical symptoms like headaches and muscle pain, and it can make us more prone to addictive behaviors like drinking alcohol.

The key is to find a balance between stress and rest, and to make sure we're taking care of our bodies and minds by replenishing the energy and nutrients we use up during stressful times. By learning to manage stress and prioritize self-care, we can achieve our goals and live happier, healthier lives.

Connect with others.

Maintaining a social life is essential for stress management, so make time to socialize with friends.

Practice mindfulness.

Mindfulness techniques involve brief meditations that direct our attention to our immediate surroundings or the task at hand.

They have been scientifically demonstrated to reduce stress and improve our overall well-being.

Happiness is an emotion, not a constant state we can achieve

Let's face it, we all want to be happy. It's what we strive for and what we're told to chase. But what if we've been chasing the wrong thing all along? What if happiness isn't a permanent state but a fleeting emotion like all the others?

According to author Russ Harris, our emotions are like the weather, always changing and sometimes pleasant and sometimes difficult. It's natural to experience emotions other than happiness, and that doesn't necessarily mean that our lives are off track or that we have a mental health problem.

Dr. Julie Smith emphasizes that fixating on happiness or why we're not happier can actually make us feel worse. Instead of chasing happiness, she suggests that we determine our personal values, which provide a framework for decision-making and motivation during difficult times.

Values are the principles that define who we want to be in life and how we want to live it. By spending time discovering our values, we can give our lives meaning and purpose beyond just seeking happiness. And in the end, isn't a life with purpose and meaning what we're all really looking for?

Identify and reframe the problems you are struggling with

"In the infinity of life where I am, all is perfect, whole, and complete, and yet life is ever changing. There is no beginning and no end, only a constant cycling and recycling of substance and experiences." - Louise Hay

Our past shapes us, and childhood traumas can lead to negative habits. To move forward, we can look to Louise Hay's positive philosophy, which she shares in her bestselling book You Can Heal Your Life. She uses her own experiences and approach to help readers change their lives through self-love.

Louise Hay discovered a curious thing when she asked her clients to talk about their problems: the details of the situation didn't always match the emotions behind them.

While some circumstances in life are out of our control, we always have power over our reactions and perspectives. To address the issues that trouble us, we must first look inward and examine different aspects of our life.

However, be careful with the word 'should,' as it can carry shame and pressure, making you feel bad about yourself.

Why do we blame ourselves for every problem in our lives? The truth is that our insecurities and shame blind us.

Learning to love ourselves can be difficult, but it is essential. It's not about ignoring our flaws, but about embracing gratitude and understanding our self-worth.

Many times, we engage in self-destructive behavior, such as drug abuse or toxic relationships, thinking we don't deserve any better. But by recognizing our value, we can start to realize that our problems don't define us as individuals.

"I continue to explain that no matter what their problem seems to be, there is only one thing I ever work on with anyone, and this is Loving the Self."
- Louise Hay

Look in the mirror and say out loud that **you accept yourself exactly as you are**. Sit with the uncomfortable feeling and repeat the words again.

The solution to most of your problems lies in forgiveness and letting go

Take charge of your life, even when it feels like everything is out of control. You have agency, and it's up to you to use it.

If you're struggling with unhealthy habits, start by being honest with yourself. It's hard to let go of toxic relationships or patterns, but it's even harder to be stuck in a cycle of pain.

Remember, your bad habits are just a symptom of something deeper. But you can change, and you're worth the effort.

Don't let your thoughts control you - you have the power to take charge of your mind and your life. It won't be easy, but it's possible. Practice and consistency are key.

You may have been taught that you're worthless or undeserving of good things, but that's simply not true.

Forgive yourself for past mistakes and let go of anger and resentment. Only then can you be present and move forward.

"Feel a warmth beginning to glow in your heart center, a softness, a gentleness. Let this feeling begin to change the way you think and talk about yourself."
- Louise Hay

Commit yourself to forgiveness.

Close your eyes and state aloud who and what you wish to forgive. Repeat this to yourself until you believe it.

Shifting your perspective can help you feel fulfilled with what you already have

"Relationships are mirrors of ourselves. What we attract always mirrors either qualities we have or beliefs we have about relationships." - Louise Hay

Have you ever noticed how the people in your life can have a big impact on how you treat yourself? It's true.

If you grew up in an environment where you were never praised for your achievements or were mistreated as a child, it can be hard to show yourself the love and care you deserve as an adult.

And unfortunately, some of us can fall into the trap of seeking out abusive partners because it feels familiar. But there's hope. You can break this cycle by recognizing your own worth and that you are deserving of love and respect.

Once you recognize that you are a complex, multidimensional being with both strengths and weaknesses, you can start to shift your perspective on your current challenges. Instead of letting your insecurities and doubts control you, take a step back and consider whether your problems are based in reality or just in your head.

This shift in perspective can help you in other areas of your life too. Maybe you're feeling stuck in a dead-end job that's underpaying and unfulfilling. But remember, it's just a stepping stone to bigger and better things.

And if you're unhappy with your appearance, it's time to start appreciating all the amazing things your body can do.

It's not uncommon for emotional turmoil to manifest as physical pain, like headaches and other aches and pains. But by recognizing your worth and letting go of anger and negativity, you can start to let go of that pain too.

Practice appreciation for everyone.

Your forgiveness and understanding should extend to everyone, including those who have wronged you.

Everyone has reasons for acting the way they do, but this is not an excuse. But it was a lesson in patience.

Hating yourself is usually a way of rejecting others

One of Kishimi's, the author of the bestselling book The courage to be disliked, students once revealed a troubling self-hatred because he was too aware of his flaws, both objective and subjective.

Objective inferiorities are those that we can confirm, like lacking height or money. But subjective ones are self-critical beliefs, often entirely fabricated.

In this instance, the young man was creating reasons to hate himself to avoid being hurt by others. Kishimi helped him realize that his loneliness was the root cause of his misery, not any actual shortcomings.

According to Adler, the only flaws we should address are the objective ones, only if they hinder us from achieving our goals. But subjective ones are mere illusions and we should examine them before deeming ourselves unworthy.

An excellent remedy for this problem is to "**love yourself like your life depends on it**," as Kamal Ravikant puts it.

This can help you embrace yourself and appreciate your unique qualities, without getting trapped in self-criticism.

Competitive mindsets destroy our mental health

Comparison is often described as the thief of joy, but it's also the gateway to misery. Mark Twain recognized this, and it's a concept that's been further developed by the 20th-century psychologist, Alfred Adler.

In Adler's view, the competitive nature of modern societies can be harmful to our mental health and wellbeing.

This is a topic that has been hotly debated in discussions on Western versus Eastern cultures. Countries like Japan and China are known for their emphasis on cooperation, whereas the U.S. and Germany tend to prioritize individualistic ideas of success.

However, the problem with a narrow, competitive mindset is that it can never truly lead to happiness. **If you believe that you need to be the best at everything to find fulfillment - whether it's making money, gaining social media likes, or having a lot of friends - you'll always feel anxious and unfulfilled.**

Adler believed that the true purpose of psychology was to help individuals become courageous. By letting go of a competitive mindset and embracing abundance, you'll never feel like anyone is holding you back.

There's enough success to go around for everyone, and as long as you focus on improving yourself, you can achieve anything.

Cooperate more with others.

Imagine life as a team sport. While individual achievements can be rewarding, working with others and accomplishing goals together is what makes the game of life truly satisfying.

Cooperation not only helps you form deeper connections with those around you but also boosts your own self-esteem. Don't let individualistic thinking limit your potential for growth and fulfillment.

Be open to receiving positive feedback and constructive criticism from others. It's a key ingredient to personal and interpersonal success. So, let go of that "me, myself, and I" mentality and embrace the power of teamwork. Together, we can achieve greatness.

THANK YOU

Dear Readers,

I want to express my heartfelt gratitude to each and every one of you who has taken the time to read my book. Your support and interest mean everything to me, and I am deeply honored that you have chosen to spend your time with my words.

Writing a book is a journey, and it's not one that can be undertaken alone. It takes a community of readers and supporters to bring a book to life, and I am so grateful to have you as a part of that community.

I hope that the ideas and insights presented in these pages have been helpful and meaningful to you. My goal in writing this book was to provide practical advice, inspiration, and food for thought, and I truly hope that it has delivered on those promises. Please share your review and feedback on Amazon and feel free to reach out to me on Instagram @bookreadersclub.

Once again, thank you from the bottom of my heart for taking the time to read my book. Your support means the world to me, and I hope that my words have made a positive impact on your life.

With gratitude and appreciation,

Shubham

OTHER BOOKS BY THE AUTHOR

Are you tired of feeling overwhelmed by life's challenges? Do you struggle with finding meaning and purpose in your daily routine?

Stoicism offers a unique and practical approach to these common problems. In "The Modern Stoic: 100 Laws for Thriving in a Chaotic World," you will find lessons from the prominent stoic thinkers Zeno of Citium, Epictetus, Seneca, and Marcus Aurelius. **These 100 laws will teach you how to live a virtuous and fulfilling life, regardless of your circumstances.**

By incorporating these stoic principles into your daily routine, you can learn to **control your emotions,**

overcome adversity, and find joy in even the most difficult situations. This book offers a comprehensive guide to understanding and applying the wisdom of the Stoics, in a way that is accessible and easy to follow.

Whether you are a seasoned practitioner of Stoicism or just beginning to explore this ancient philosophy, "The Modern Stoic" will provide you with practical insights and tools for living a life of wisdom, courage, and resilience.

So why wait? Start your journey towards a more fulfilling life today!

ADDITIONAL RESOURCES

As a thank you to our readers, we've compiled a list of books that inspired the writing of Good Books Gone Bad. We hope these additional resources will provide even more insights and inspiration on your journey to personal growth and self-improvement.

Here are the books and their respective authors that influenced our writing:

1. The Power of Now by Eckhart Tolle - A spiritual guidebook that emphasizes the importance of living in the present moment.

2. Buddha's Brain by Rick Hanson - A neuroscience-based book that explores the intersection of modern psychology and Buddhist teachings.

3. The Art of Happiness by Dalai Lama XIV and Howard C. Cutler - A practical and philosophical guide to finding inner peace and happiness.

4. How to Connect by Thich Nhat Hanh - A guide to cultivating compassionate relationships and deepening our connections with others.

5. How to Love by Thich Nhat Hanh - A collection of teachings on how to love and be loved, focusing on mindfulness and compassion.

6. Four Thousand Weeks by Oliver Burkeman - A philosophical exploration of how we can make the most of our limited time on earth.

7. Atomic Habits by James Clear - A practical guide to building and breaking habits, focusing on small, incremental changes.

8. The 7 Habits of Highly Effective People by Stephen R. Covey - A classic self-help book that provides a comprehensive framework for personal and professional success.

9. The Compound Effect by Darren Hardy - A book that emphasizes the power of small, consistent actions in achieving our goals and building momentum.

10. The Subtle Art of Not Giving a F*ck by Mark Manson - A self-help book that challenges readers to reexamine their priorities and stop sweating the small stuff.

11. Ikigai by Héctor García and Francesc Miralles - A book that explores the Japanese concept of ikigai, or "reason for being," and how to find purpose and fulfillment in life.

12. Rich Dad Poor Dad by Robert Kiyosaki - A personal finance book that encourages readers to think differently about money and investing.

13. Stolen Focus by Colleen M. Story - A guide to managing distractions and staying focused in a world full of competing demands.

14. Man's Search for Meaning by Viktor E. Frankl - A memoir and psychological treatise that explores the human capacity for finding meaning and purpose in the face of suffering.

15. Letters from a Stoic by Seneca - A collection of philosophical letters that offers practical advice on how to live a virtuous and fulfilling life.

16. How to Be Free by Joe Blow - A book that offers practical advice on how to break free from self-imposed limitations and live a more fulfilling life.

17. Thinking, Fast and Slow by Daniel Kahneman - A book that explores the two systems of thinking that govern our decision-making processes and how we can improve them.

18. Influence by Robert Cialdini - A classic book on the principles of persuasion and how to use them ethically in our personal and professional lives.

19. Think Again by Adam Grant - A book that challenges readers to reexamine their beliefs and biases and develop a more open-minded and flexible approach to life.

20. The 5am Club by Robin Sharma - A self-help book that promotes the benefits of waking up early and adopting a morning routine.

21. Why Has Nobody Told Me This Before? by Dr. Julie Smith - A book that offers practical advice on how to manage mental health.

22. How to Heal Your Life? by Louise L. Hay - A self-help book that offers practical advice on how to improve our physical, emotional, and spiritual well-being.

23. The Courage to Be Disliked by Ichiro Kishimi and Fumitake Koga - A philosophical dialogue that explores the teachings of Alfred Adler and how to live a fulfilling life based on our own unique values and goals.

We hope these additional resources provide you with even more valuable insights and ideas.

Thank you again for reading Good Books Gone Bad.

Made in the USA
Las Vegas, NV
25 September 2023

78110635R10101